W9-CRZ-582

BODY WORKS™

HEART

Shannon Caster

PowerKiDS
press

New York

For my former students at Legacy Point and Iron Horse Elementary

Published in 2010 by The Rosen Publishing Group, Inc.
29 East 21st Street, New York, NY 10010

First Edition

Editor: Joanne Randolph
Book Design: Greg Tucker
Layout Design: Kate Laczynski
Photo Researcher: Jessica Gerweck

Photo Credits: Cover, p. 9 3D Clinic/Getty Images; pp. 5, 10, 17 3D4Medical.com/Getty Images; p. 5 (inset) © www.istockphoto.com/Vlad Turchenko; pp. 6, 13 (inset) Nucleus Medical Art, Inc./Getty Images; pp. 10 (inset), 13, 14, 18 Shutterstock.com; p. 14 (inset) Dorling Kindersley/Getty Images; p. 17 (inset) Vicky Kasala/Getty Images; p. 18 (inset) Yorgos Nikas/Getty Images; p. 21 Rebecca Emery/Getty Images.

Library of Congress Cataloging-in-Publication Data

Caster, Shannon.
  Heart / Shannon Caster. — 1st ed.
      p. cm. — (Body works)
  Includes index.
  ISBN 978-1-4358-9370-2 (library binding) — ISBN 978-1-4358-9828-8 (pbk.) — ISBN 978-1-4358-9829-5 (6-pack)
  1. Heart—Juvenile literature. 2. Cardiovascular system—Juvenile literature. I. Title.
  QP111.6.C37 2010
  612.1'7—dc22

2009034088

Manufactured in the United States of America

CPSIA Compliance Information: Batch #WW10PK: For Further Information contact Rosen Publishing, New York, New York at 1-800-237-9932

Contents

Put Your Heart into It!

Try jumping up and down in place for a minute. Now put your hand on your chest. That thumping you feel is your heart beating. The extra exercise from jumping made your heart **pump** faster than normal.

Your heart is a strong **muscle** located near the middle of your chest. Your heart works nonstop, 24 hours a day. Every minute, your heart pumps about 5 quarts (5 l) of blood to your body through a **network** of **blood vessels**. Together, your heart, blood vessels, and blood make up your body's cardiovascular system.

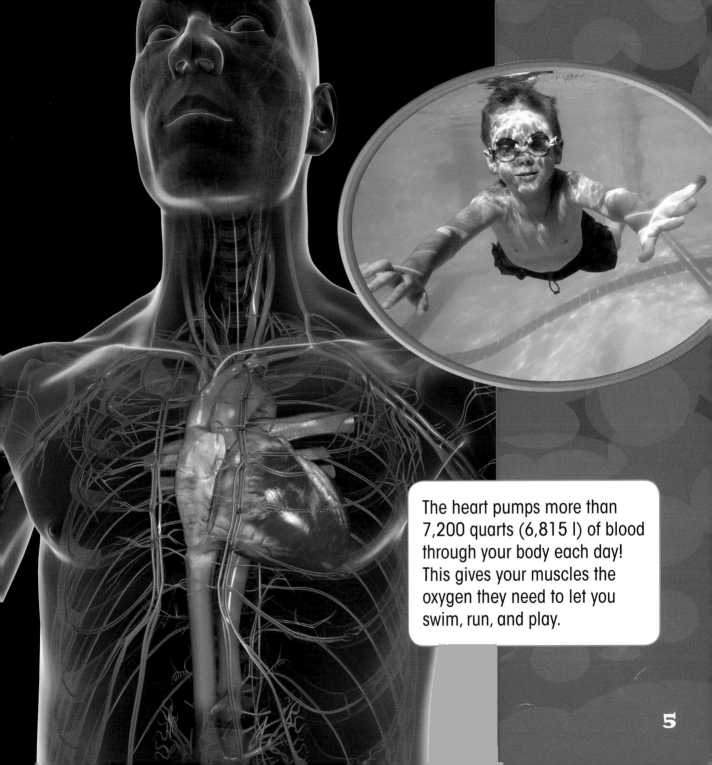

The heart pumps more than 7,200 quarts (6,815 l) of blood through your body each day! This gives your muscles the oxygen they need to let you swim, run, and play.

Here you can see the four chambers of the heart. The septum is the thick pink wall that passes through the center of the heart.

Right Atrium

Left Atrium

Right Ventricle

Left Ventricle

Through the Chambers

Your heart is divided into four chambers, or spaces. The top two chambers are the right **atrium** and the left atrium. The bottom two chambers are the right and left **ventricles**. A thick muscular wall called a septum separates the right side of the heart from the left. The septum keeps blood in the right side from mixing with blood in the left side. The part of the septum that separates the atria is called the atrial septum. The part that separates the ventricles is called the ventricular septum.

Blood from the body flows into the right atrium. After the blood travels around the heart, the left ventricle pumps it back into the body.

Holding Rooms

The right and left atria collect blood coming into the heart. When the atria fill up, they push blood into the ventricles.

The right atrium collects blood returning from the body. This blood is **oxygen** poor, or has very little oxygen in it. This is because cells in the body have used the oxygen for **energy**.

This oxygen-poor blood moves from the right atrium into the right ventricle, which pushes the blood into the **lungs**. The blood gets rid of waste gases in the lungs and picks up oxygen. Blood moves from the lungs to the left atrium, then into the left ventricle.

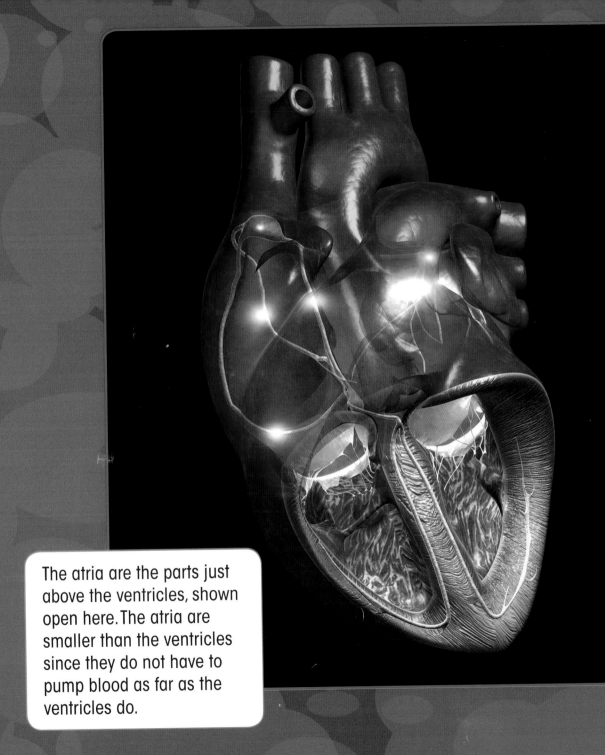

The atria are the parts just above the ventricles, shown open here. The atria are smaller than the ventricles since they do not have to pump blood as far as the ventricles do.

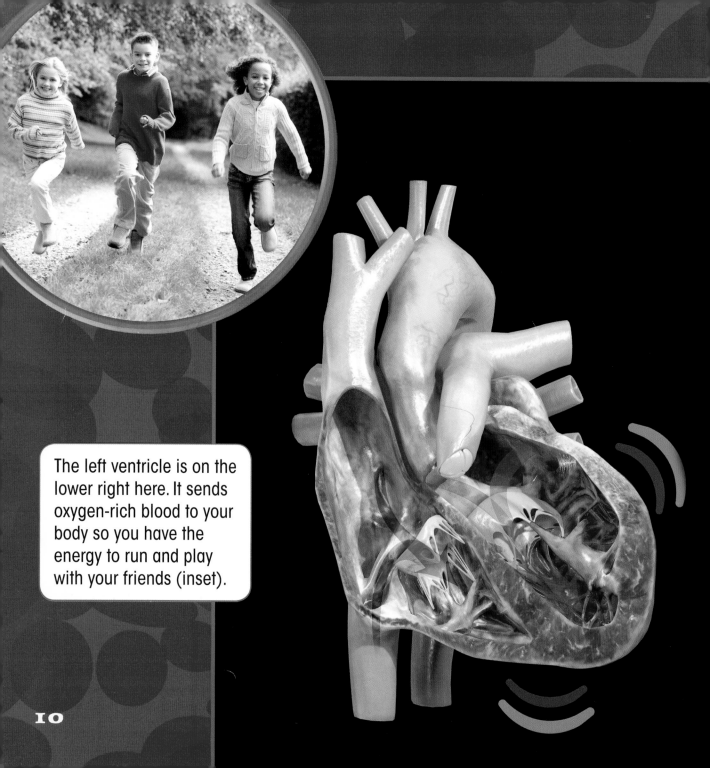

The left ventricle is on the lower right here. It sends oxygen-rich blood to your body so you have the energy to run and play with your friends (inset).

Pumping Stations

The ventricles are the largest chambers in the heart. They act like pumping stations, pushing blood out of the heart. In order to **contract** with enough power, the ventricles have very thick muscular walls. The walls press together and blood is pushed through the top of the heart.

The right ventricle is in charge of pumping oxygen-poor blood to the lungs, where it picks up more oxygen. The left ventricle pumps oxygen-rich blood that has returned from the lungs to the rest of the body. The left ventricle is the strongest part of the heart, since it needs to be able to push blood around the whole body.

Heart Valves

Each heart chamber has one valve, or door. The names of the valves inside the heart are the tricuspid, the pulmonary, the mitral, and the aortic valves. When a chamber contracts, the valve opens to allow blood to flow out. After the blood flows out, the valves shut tightly again. The closing of the valves keeps blood from flowing backward through the heart. As the valves open and close, we get the "lub-dub" sound of our heartbeat.

When a doctor listens to your heart through a **stethoscope**, this "lub-dub" sound is what she is trying to hear. It lets her know that blood is moving through the heart as it should.

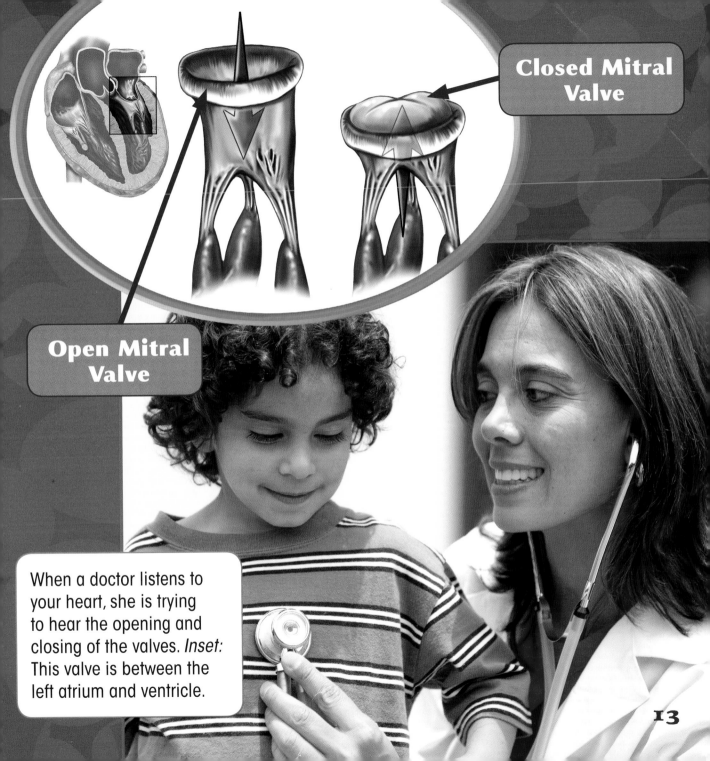

Closed Mitral Valve

Open Mitral Valve

When a doctor listens to your heart, she is trying to hear the opening and closing of the valves. *Inset:* This valve is between the left atrium and ventricle.

13

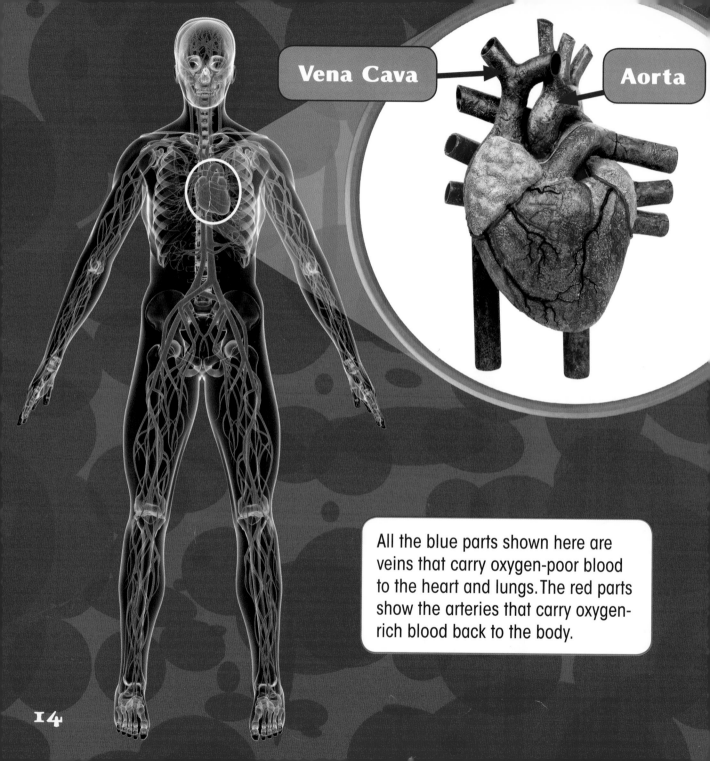

Vena Cava

Aorta

All the blue parts shown here are veins that carry oxygen-poor blood to the heart and lungs. The red parts show the arteries that carry oxygen-rich blood back to the body.

Leaving the Heart

Your body has a network of blood vessels that carry blood to and from the heart. The vessels that bring blood to the heart are called veins. The vessels that move blood away from the heart are called arteries. Arteries carry oxygen-rich blood to capillaries in every part of your body. The capillaries, which are tiny blood vessels, then push oxygen-poor blood into the veins, which carry it back to the heart and lungs.

The aorta, at the top of the heart, is the body's largest artery. Oxygen-rich blood enters the aorta from the left ventricle then branches off into smaller arteries.

To the Lungs

Like the aorta, the pulmonary artery carries blood away from the heart. However, the pulmonary artery is different from the other arteries in the body. It is the only artery to carry oxygen-poor blood. That is usually the veins' job!

The pulmonary artery takes blood away from the right ventricle and carries it to the lungs. The pulmonary artery breaks off into two branches. One branch carries blood to the right lung. The other branch carries blood to the left lung. Once blood reaches the lungs, it can pick up oxygen to power the body again.

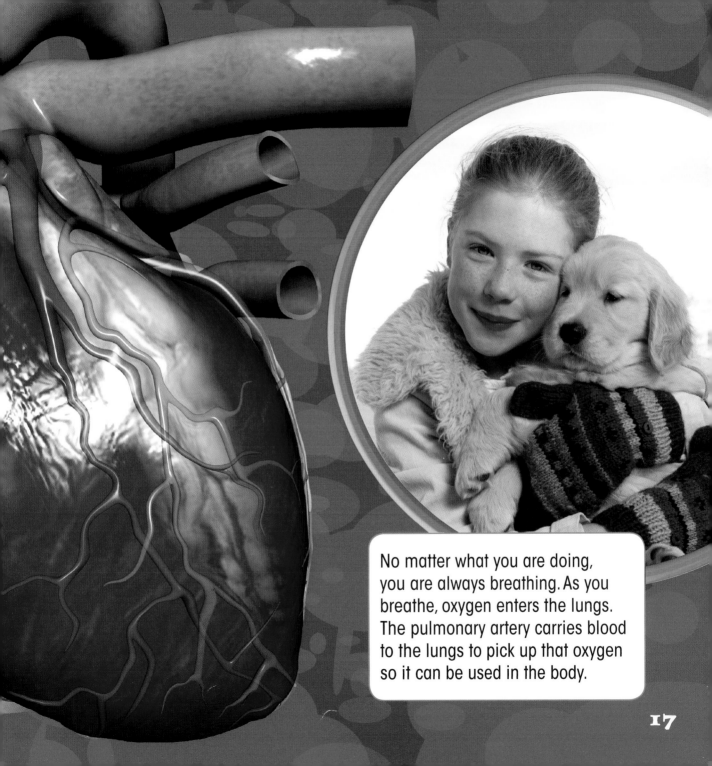

No matter what you are doing, you are always breathing. As you breathe, oxygen enters the lungs. The pulmonary artery carries blood to the lungs to pick up that oxygen so it can be used in the body.

When you get a cut, blood cleans it out, and then platelets stop the bleeding. *Inset:* Here you can see the different parts of your blood.

Platelet

Red Blood Cell

White Blood Cell

Up Close: The Blood

Your heart and blood work as a team. Your heart pumps blood that is carrying oxygen and **nutrients** to your body. Once the oxygen is used up, the blood returns to your heart and lungs to pick up more oxygen. Without oxygen, your body's cells would die.

Blood is made up of different kinds of cells that float in a yellow, watery matter, called plasma. Red blood cells carry the oxygen in your blood. White blood cells fight off illness. Platelets help the blood clot, or stop bleeding, when you get a cut. All these parts of your blood work together to keep your body alive and healthy.

The Pressure!

Touch your first two fingers to the inside of your wrist and feel your **pulse**. As the heart beats, it pushes blood through your arteries. Each push can be felt or heard as a pulse. If your heart beats 80 times in a minute, you will feel 80 pulses.

Blood pressure is the measure of how hard the heart is pushing blood through your arteries. When the heart contracts, it pushes blood the hardest. When the heart relaxes, the pressure is less on the arterial walls. Doctors take your blood pressure as a measure of your heart's health. High blood pressure can mean your heart is working too hard.

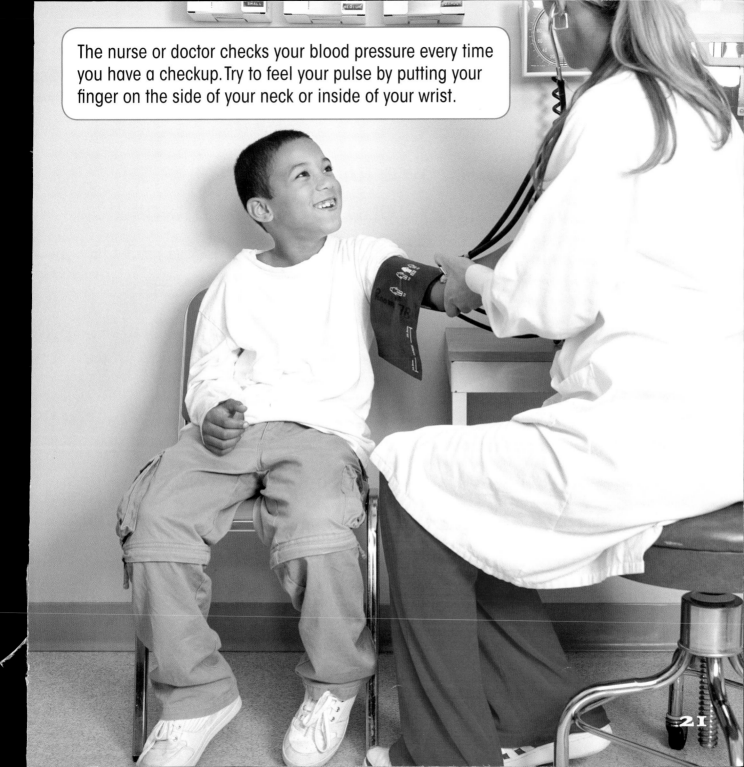

The nurse or doctor checks your blood pressure every time you have a checkup. Try to feel your pulse by putting your finger on the side of your neck or inside of your wrist.

Heart Trouble

The heart is a powerful muscle that sometimes runs into trouble. A heart attack occurs when not enough blood and oxygen get to your heart. If fat builds up in your arteries, the space inside the arteries becomes smaller. Then a blood clot can block the blood trying to flow through.

Without a rich supply of blood and oxygen, the heart stops working. The heart muscle can be hurt, or even die, if the blood supply is not renewed. By eating healthy foods and exercising, you can help your blood vessels and your heart keep working smoothly.

Glossary

atrium (AY-tree-um) A heart chamber that takes in blood from the body.

blood vessels (BLUD VEH-sulz) Narrow tubes in the body through which blood flows.

contract (kun-TRAKT) To pull together and tighten.

energy (EH-nur-jee) The power to work or to act.

lungs (LUNGZ) The parts of an air-breathing animal that take in air and supply oxygen to the blood.

muscle (MUH-sul) A part of the body that makes the body move.

network (NET-wurk) A system or group of things that connect to each other.

nutrients (NOO-tree-unts) Food that a living thing needs to live and grow.

oxygen (OK-sih-jen) A gas that has no color or taste and is necessary for people and animals to breathe.

pulse (PULS) A single beat, sound, or throb.

pump (PUMP) To remove liquid, or watery matter, from one place and move it to another.

stethoscope (STETH-uh-skohp) A tool used to listen to a heartbeat.

ventricles (VEN-trih-kulz) Chambers of the heart from which blood is pumped to the body.

Index

A
arteries, 15–16, 20, 22
atrium, 7–8

B
blood vessels, 4, 15, 22
body, 4, 7–8, 11, 15–16, 19

C
cardiovascular system, 4
cells, 8, 19
chamber(s), 7, 11–12
chest, 4

E
energy, 8
exercise, 4

L
lung(s), 8, 11, 15–16

M
muscle, 4, 22

N
network, 4, 15
nutrients, 19

O
oxygen, 8, 11, 16, 19, 22

P
part(s), 7, 15, 19
power, 11
pulse, 20

S
septum, 7
stethoscope, 12

V
veins, 15
ventricle(s), 7–8, 11, 15–16

W
wall(s), 7, 11, 20
waste gases, 8

Web Sites

Due to the changing nature of Internet links, PowerKids Press has developed an online list of Web sites related to the subject of this book. This site is updated regularly. Please use this link to access the list:
www.powerkidslinks.com/hybw/heart/